PRESENTED TO

BY

ON

Read *With* Me   Bible Series

Kids of the Bible

Illustrated by
Dennis Jones

Edited by
Catherine DeVries

Zondervan Publishing House
Grand Rapids, Michigan

Contents

The First Babies 8
Boy Saved by a Ram 10
Twin Brothers 12
Joseph's Colorful Coat 14
Baby Moses 16
Moses Grows Up—in a Palace! 18
No Haircuts for Samson! 20
Samuel Hears God Calling Him 22
David Kills a Giant 24
Boy Sneezes and Comes Back to Life! 26
An Eight-Year-Old King! 28
Infants and Children Praise God 30
Remember Your Creator 32
Children Are a Gift 34

God Made Me 36
A Crown to Older People 38
Friends of Wild Animals 40
This Boy Ate Locusts and Honey 42
How Baby Jesus Was Born 44
At Age 12 Jesus Knew More Than Teachers 46
Boy Healed by Jesus 48
Little Girl Comes Back to Life 50
Boy Gives His Lunch to Jesus—Feeds 5,000! . . . 52
Children Free of Pride 54
Children Come to Jesus 56
Children Shout, "Hosanna!" 58
Be a Leader! 60
We're All Children of God 62

The First Babies

Genesis 4:1–2

Cain and Abel were the first human babies in the whole world! Their parents, Adam and Eve, were the first mom and dad in the whole world.

When they grew up, Abel took care of sheep and Cain worked the ground.

Boy Saved by a Ram

Genesis 22:2–3, 7–9, 11–13

God told Abraham to take his only son and go to Mount Moriah. "Give him to me there as an offering," said God. So Abraham and his son Isaac went to the place. Isaac said, "Father, the fire and wood are here. But where is the lamb for the offering?" Abraham replied, "God himself will provide the lamb." Abraham built an altar and arranged the wood on it. He tied up his son and placed him on top of the wood. Then an angel called out to Abraham from heaven and told him to stop. "Now I know that you have respect for God. You have not held back from me your only son," said the angel. Abraham looked up and saw a ram in a bush. It was caught by its horns. He sacrificed the ram on the altar.

Twin Brothers

Genesis 25:21, 24–27

Rebekah couldn't have children. Her husband Isaac prayed to the LORD for her. And the LORD answered his prayer. Rebekah became pregnant and had twin boys. The first one to be born was red and his whole body was covered with hair. So they named him Esau. Then his brother was born. His hand was holding onto Esau's heel. So he was named Jacob.

The boys grew up. Esau became a skillful hunter. He liked the open country. But Jacob was a quiet man. He stayed at home among the tents.

Joseph's Colorful Coat

Genesis 37:3–4

Israel loved Joseph more than any of his other sons. Israel made him a beautiful robe. Joseph's brothers saw that their father loved him more than any of them. So they hated Joseph. They couldn't even speak one kind word to him.

Baby Moses

Exodus 1:22; 2:1–4

When Moses was a baby, his mother hid him from Pharaoh. Pharaoh wanted to get rid of him and all the other Hebrew baby boys. When Moses' mother could hide him no longer, she got a basket made out of the stems of tall grass. She coated it with tar. Then she placed the child in it. She put the basket in the tall grass along the bank of the Nile River. God kept Moses safe. The child's sister wasn't very far away. She wanted to see what would happen to Moses.

Moses Grows Up—in a Palace!

Exodus 2:5–10

Pharaoh's daughter went down to the Nile River to take a bath. She saw baby Moses in the basket. He was crying, and she felt sorry for him. The baby's sister had been watching from the river bank. She asked the princess, "Do you want me to go and get one of the Hebrew women? She could nurse the baby for you." The princess answered, "Yes, go." So the girl went and got Moses' mother. She took back her baby and nursed him. When Moses grew older, the princess took him to live in Pharaoh's palace. And he became her son.

No Haircuts for Samson!

Judges 13:3, 5, 24–25; 16:13, 19

Samson was a special gift from God. An angel told his parents that from the day he was born, he would be "set apart to God." The angel said that Samson's hair should never be cut.

As Samson grew up, the LORD blessed him. He was very, very strong. The Spirit of the LORD began to work in Samson's life. And his hair grew and grew. He wore it in seven long braids until some bad people cut it when Samson was a grown-up. As soon as they cut it, Samson lost his strength.

Samuel Hears God Calling Him

1 Samuel 3:2–5, 8–10, 12, 20

A boy named Samuel lived in the LORD's House with a priest named Eli. One night when they were lying down to sleep, the LORD called out to Samuel. Samuel ran over to Eli and said, "Here I am. You called out to me." But Eli said, "I didn't call you. Go back and lie down." This very same thing happened two more times. Then the priest realized that the LORD was calling the boy.

Eli told Samuel, "Go and lie down. If someone calls out to you again, say, 'Speak, LORD. I'm listening.'" Samuel went and lay down in his place. The LORD came and stood there and called out to him again. Samuel replied, "Speak. I'm listening." The LORD told Samuel what would happen to Eli and his sons. Samuel became a prophet of the LORD.

22

David Kills a Giant

1 Samuel 17:4, 8–9, 32–33, 37, 40, 45, 49

Goliath was more than nine feet tall! He dared any man from Israel's army to come fight him. David was a shepherd boy. He wanted to fight Goliath, but King Saul said, "You are too young." David replied, "The LORD will save me from this Philistine." Then David picked up his wooden staff. He went down to a stream and chose five smooth stones. Then he took his sling in his hand and approached Goliath. "You are coming to fight against me with a sword, a spear and a javelin," he said. "But I'm coming against you in the name of the LORD who rules over all." David put a stone in his sling and he slung it at Goliath. The stone hit Goliath on the forehead and sank into it. He fell to the ground on his face!

Boy Sneezes
and Comes Back to Life!

2 Kings 4:9–10, 20, 25, 27, 32–35

A woman's son died. She went to find her friend Elisha, the man of God. Elisha visited her and her family so often that he had his own bedroom at their house. The woman found Elisha at Mount Carmel. She took hold of his feet. Elisha knew she was suffering and went with her back to her house. The boy was lying on Elisha's bed. Elisha went into the room and shut the door. He prayed to the LORD and then warmed the boy's body two times. His eyes touched the boy's eyes. His hands touched the boy's hands. The boy sneezed seven times. After that, he opened his eyes. He was alive again!

An Eight-Year-Old King!

2 Kings 22:1–2, 5–6; 23:25

Josiah was eight years old when he became king, and he ruled in Jerusalem 31 years. Josiah did what was right in the eyes of the LORD. Josiah ordered that the temple of the LORD be rebuilt and that God's people should once again obey God's rules. There was no king like Josiah either before him or after him.

Infants and Children Praise God

Psalm 8:1–2

LORD, our Lord, how majestic is your name in the whole earth! You have made your glory higher than the heavens. You have made sure that children and infants praise you.

Remember Your Creator

Psalm 65:9, 12–13

God, you take care of the land and water it. You make it very rich. You fill your streams with water. The hills are dressed with gladness. The meadows are covered with flocks and herds. The valleys are dressed with grain. They sing and shout with joy.

Ecclesiastes 12:1

Remember the One who created you. Remember him while you are still young.

Children Are a Gift

Psalm 127:3–5

Children are a gift from the LORD. They are a reward from him. Sons who are born to people when they are young are like arrows in the hands of a soldier. Blessed is the man who has many children.

God Made Me

Psalm 139:1, 13–14, 16–18

LORD, you know all about me. You put me together inside my mother's body. How you made me is amazing and wonderful. I praise you for that. You planned how many days I would live. God, your thoughts about me are priceless. No one can possibly add them all up. If I could count them, they would be more than the grains of sand.

A Crown to Older People

Proverbs 17:6

Grandchildren are like a crown to older people. And children are proud of their parents.

Friends of Wild Animals

Isaiah 11:6–7, 9, 11

One day the Lord will reach out his hand to gather his people. Wolves will live with lambs. Leopards will lie down with goats. Calves and lions will eat together. And little children will lead them around. Cows will eat with bears. Their little ones will lie down together. None of those animals will harm or destroy anything or anyone. The earth will be filled with the knowledge of the LORD.

This Boy Ate Locusts and Honey

Matthew 3:4–6; Mark 1:5; Luke 1:76

John's clothes were made out of camel's hair. He had a leather belt around his waist. His food was locusts and wild honey. He lived in the desert. People went out to him from Jerusalem and all of Judea. They also came from the whole area around the Jordan River. When they admitted they had sinned, John baptized them in the Jordan.

John went ahead of the Lord [Jesus] to prepare the way for him.

How Baby Jesus Was Born

Matthew 1:18, 20–21

Mary and Joseph had promised to get married. But before they started to live together, it was clear that she was going to have a baby. An angel said to Joseph, "Don't be afraid to take Mary home as your wife. The baby inside her is from the Holy Spirit. You must name the baby Jesus. He will save his people from their sins."

At Age 12 Jesus Knew More Than Teachers

Luke 2:41–47

Every year Jesus and his parents went to Jerusalem for the Passover Feast. When Jesus was 12 years old, they went up to the Feast as usual. After the Feast was over, Jesus' parents left to go back home. But Jesus wasn't with them. Joseph and Mary looked for him among their relatives and friends. But they did not find him! So they went back to Jerusalem. After three days they found him with the teachers in the temple courtyard. He was listening to them and asking them questions. Everyone who heard him was amazed at how much Jesus understood. They also were amazed at his answers.

Boy Healed by Jesus

John 4:46–47, 50–53

A royal official went to Jesus and begged him to come and heal his son. The boy was close to death. Jesus said to the official, "You may go. Your son will live." The man believed what Jesus said, and so he left. While the man was still on his way home, his servants met him. They gave him the news that his boy was living. He asked what time his son got better. They said to him, "The fever left him yesterday afternoon at one o'clock." That was the exact time Jesus had said to him, "Your son will live." So the man and all his family became believers.

Little Girl Comes Back to Life

Mark 5:35–36, 38–42

Jairus was a synagogue ruler. Some men from his house came to bring him sad news. "Your daughter is dead," they said. But Jesus told Jairus, "Don't be afraid. Just believe." They went to his house. There people were crying and sobbing loudly. Jesus said, "Why all this confusion and sobbing? The child is not dead. She is only sleeping." But they laughed at him. He made them all go outside. Jesus took only the child's father and mother and the disciples who were with him. And he went in to where the child was. Jesus took her by the hand. Then he said to her, "Little girl, I say to you, get up!" The girl was 12 years old. Right away she stood up and walked around!

Boy Gives His Lunch to Jesus—Feeds 5,000!

John 6:5, 8–11, 13

Jesus saw a large crowd coming toward him. He said to Philip, "Where can we buy bread for these people to eat?" Andrew, Simon Peter's brother, said, "Here is a boy with five small loaves of barley bread and two small fish. But how far will that go in such a large crowd?" Jesus said, "Have the people sit down." The number of men among them was about 5,000 plus women and children. Jesus took the loaves and gave thanks. He handed out the bread to those who were seated. He gave them as much as they wanted. And he did the same with the fish. All of them had enough to eat. There were even 12 baskets of leftovers!

Children Free of Pride

Matthew 18:3–4

Jesus said, "What I'm about to tell you is true. You need to change and become like little children. If you don't, you will never enter the kingdom of heaven. Anyone who becomes as free of pride as this child is the most important in the kingdom of heaven."

Children Come to Jesus

Mark 10:13–14

People were bringing little children to Jesus. They wanted him to touch them. But the disciples told the people to stop. When Jesus saw this, he was angry. He said to his disciples, "Let the little children come to me. Don't keep them away. God's kingdom belongs to people like them."

Children Shout, "Hosanna!"

Matthew 21:7–9, 15

Jesus rode into Jerusalem on a donkey. A very large crowd spread their coats on the road. Others cut branches from the trees and spread them on the road. They all shouted, "Hosanna to the Son of David! Blessed is he who comes in the name of the Lord!" The children in the temple area were shouting, "Hosanna to the Son of David!" Hosanna means "save us."

Be a Leader!

1 Timothy 4:12

Don't let anyone look down on you because you are young. Set an example for the believers in what you say and in how you live. Also set an example in how you love and in what you believe.

We're All Children of God

1 John 3:1

How great is the love the Father has given us so freely! Now we can be called children of God. And that's what we really are!

Project Management and Editorial: **Catherine DeVries**
Interior Art and Cover Art: **Dennis Jones**
Interior Design: **Sue Vandenberg Koppenol**
Cover Design: **Jody Langley**
Printing: **Quebecor Printing, Kingsport, TN**